Thank God for the Feedback*

USING FEEDBACK TO FUEL YOUR PERSONAL, PROFESSIONAL AND SPIRITUAL GROWTH

even when it's off-base, unfair, poorly delivered, and, frankly, you're not in the mood

WORKBOOK

SHEILA HEEN
& ELAINE LIN

speck books

Published by speck, llc.
Cambridge, Massachusetts

ISBN 978-0692493434

We wish to thank Ann Garrido, Mike Garrido, Joyce Heen, Jack Heen, Michael Baratta, Mary Jane Ashman, Marilyn Heelan, Karen Mitchell, Audrie Wright, David Eckman, Heather Kulp, Amy Hou, Grace Nicolette and Heather Sulejman for their willingness to read drafts, try out sessions, and offer theology advice. We are ever grateful for their careful reading, thoughtful suggestions, and terrific insights.

As you participate in your Small Group Study, you will develop insights and suggestions of your own for improving this Workbook. Please share these suggestions with us, so that we can incorporate your coaching into later editions of this guide and allow others to benefit from your experience.

You can send your observations — anything that you found helpful, and suggestions for improvement — to us at feedback@speckbooks.com.

CONTENTS

Introduction

The goal of this workbook, along with *Thanks for the Feedback* (by Stone and Heen), is to nurture your ability to handle the feedback coming at you – direct or indirect, spoken or unspoken – and use it to fuel your personal, professional and spiritual growth.

As Christians, we need to figure out how to handle the feedback coming at us graciously – whether from a co-worker, boss, neighbor, friend or family member. How do we handle feedback in ways that help strengthen – rather than fracture – the relationship, even when the feedback is upsetting or just seems wrong?

As Christians, we also wonder: Is *God* trying to speak to us in the feedback we get from others? What if we treated others' complaints, criticisms, or unsolicited advice as catalysts for spiritual growth – despite the unlikely messenger? It is easy to dismiss an insight – if it's offered by someone who doesn't share our values, or the way they shared it was unloving and arrogant, or because it's coming at an inconvenient or unexpected time.

Our prayer is that this study helps on both of these fronts.

Working through these questions together as a group enables you to share the struggle – the struggle to see ourselves accurately, to figure out which voices to listen to, and to get beyond defensiveness or denial in order to learn and grow. And yes, to grow even from feedback that is unfair, off-base, poorly delivered or comes when you're not in the mood. After all, while you will have a handful of gifted teachers or mentors in your life, mostly we get feedback from all the *other* people in our lives. Your boss, your sister, your teammate, your spouse, your in-laws, your customer, the guy in the SUV behind you. These people have a host of ideas on how you can upgrade your performance or personality, even while they may be terrible at offering feedback. Where in these interactions – however frustrating – might we find God, and see Him working in us?

At the end of the day, the feedback itself might or might not be right. But the *process* of understanding it, sorting it out, and deciding what to do about it is where we find opportunities to learn and grow in life, in love, in faith and in purity.

How to Use This Workbook

Before Session 1

- Purchase *Thanks for the Feedback: The Science and Art of Receiving Feedback Well (Even When It's Off-Base, Unfair, Poorly Delivered, and Frankly, You're Not in the Mood)* by Stone & Heen (Penguin 2015) and this workbook.
- Read the Introduction and Chapter 2 of *Thanks for the Feedback* (which we will refer to as TFTF in this workbook).
- Bring your Bible, the TFTF book, and this workbook to each session.

Throughout the Study

- The order of session topics in the study is different from the order of chapters in the TFTF book. In this study we have charted a path that a group might find helpful to follow as they get to know themselves and each other. Pay attention to the book chapters that correspond to each session, since they will often be read out of order.
- Group members will often be so engaged by the discussion that you may feel reluctant to move on. We encourage you to keep the conversation moving, and to continue these conversations and self-reflection after the session and during the week. The continued conversations will enrich all of your relationships – in your personal life and your professional life – and spread the benefits beyond the group, while helping you grow in all domains.
- For those interested in conducting a similar set of conversations in a secular setting – taking the format offered here into their work team, to their HR or leadership development program – a *Team Leader Guide* is available at www.stoneandheen.com.
- For those leading or facilitating the group, we have included a *Leader's Guide* at the back of this workbook. The *Leader's Guide* includes logistical reminders so that you are set up and ready for each session, as well as advice on facilitating good discussion, and substantive background that may be helpful. You will want to take a look at the corresponding session notes before you lead each of the sessions.

Group Guidelines
for Rich Discussion

Hold each other with patience and compassion.
This study invites each of you to reflect on the feedback you are getting from the most important people in your life, your emotional reactions to it, and to use it as a catalyst for growth. While growth can be exhilarating, the feedback we get from others can also be enormously painful, surprising, or just plain wrong. As you listen to *others* wrestle with their feedback, resist the temptation to jump in to agree or disagree with difficult feedback they have received ("that's just not true about you" or "well, you *can* be pretty bossy"). Your role isn't to rush or direct their journey, but to walk alongside them on it.

Remember – your reactions to each other *are* feedback.
How you react to others' comments, insights, or views *is* feedback – explicit or implicit – that can feel either supportive or judgmental.

Appreciate each other.
Support each other by recognizing the hard work others are doing to understand themselves or the material, to wrestle with difficult feedback, to bear with each other through the hard parts. Appreciation can be explicit and direct ("I really appreciate your willingness to share that with us") or indirect ("Wow.") It can also be non-verbal – a comforting hand on their arm, or a smile across the room, or an offer to spend time together during the week.

Listen always; Offer coaching only if requested.
In our efforts to "be supportive" we often jump to problem-solving – offering advice on how they can *fix* the situation. But often what is most needed is just a listening ear as they share their hurt or frustration, or sort out what they think themselves. Resist the temptation to offer them suggestions unless specifically requested.

Respect confidentiality.
People may reveal difficult moments, secret reactions, or provide an inside view of troubled relationships. Don't repeat anything shared in the group with anyone outside the group, including your spouse or significant other. Ask each member of the group to explicitly indicate their commitment to respecting confidentiality.

Balance airtime.
Remember that some people are more comfortable and quicker to speak up in a group. Others will wait for a longer pause in discussion before offering their thoughts. Share responsibility for including all voices over time, and be mindful of when you may be dominating discussion.

Be punctual and prepared.
Come prepared, having read the assigned chapters and thought about their application to your life. Arrive early so that you are seated and ready to go a few minutes before the beginning of the session.

Receive feedback graciously.
We all occasionally do things that hurt others – usually unintentionally. Invite others in the group to let you know if you inadvertently interrupt them, misunderstand what they are saying, or fall into advising or judging.

This group itself can be a wonderful practicing ground for getting better at receiving feedback from each other.

Session 1:
WHAT IS "FEEDBACK?"

AND WHAT KINDS DO I NEED TO GROW?

To Prepare:
Read TFTF Introduction & Chapter 2

> **Whoever loves discipline loves knowledge,**
> **But he who hates correction is stupid.**
>
> **Proverbs 12:1**

INTRODUCTION

When we talk about "feedback" we're talking not just about performance reviews or your relationship with your tennis coach. We're talking about all of the information you get about yourself – spoken and unspoken, direct and indirect. As you read in the Introduction to TFTF, feedback is the awkward silence after your comment in this morning's meeting, the crankiness your lateness induced in your in-laws, the delight on your second grader's face when you helped in her classroom (and the eye roll you got when your sixth grader saw you in the hall).

Scripture is filled with admonitions, examples, and exhortations for us to pay attention to feedback, and to see it as a catalyst for self-reflection, knowledge, and wisdom. Proverbs abounds with advice about how we should and should not respond to correction, from God or from those around us. Proverbs alone addresses feedback sixteen times using the word "reproof" or "reprove," five times as "rebuke," and six as "correct" or "correction." A fool ignores even the most persistent (and pounding) efforts to turn him from his ways, while a wise man loves reproof, and provides it in love.

In the English language the term "feedback" is used to describe three very different things: Appreciation, Coaching, and Evaluation (ACE). Each has a different purpose, and we actually need all three – in different amounts and at different times – in order to learn and grow. In this session we explore the distinction between the types of feedback and look for how you might invite more of the types of feedback you're wanting.

GROWING CONNECTED (15-20 minutes)

1. Share your name, what you hope to gain from the group and the study, and a few words about *how feedback was handled in your family of origin*.

2. Go around the room inviting each person to read aloud one of the "Good Guidelines for Rich Discussion."

STARTERS (15 minutes)

ACE: Your Feedback Diet
If needed, refer to the chart on page 35 of *Thanks for the Feedback*, which summarizes each type of feedback.

1. On a scale of 1 to 4, rate the quantity and quality of the appreciation, coaching, or evaluation you are currently receiving in your life. 1 is low; 4 is high.

    If it helps, you can choose a particular context (like your work team) or relationship (your spouse, family member, or a good friend).

Appreciation	1	2	3	4
Coaching	1	2	3	4
Evaluation	1	2	3	4

2. You have just *evaluated* your current feedback diet. Now give yourself some *coaching*.

    - What kind of feedback would you like *more* of in this relationship or context?

    - Who might be able to provide you with that feedback, and how might you go about asking for it?

BIBLE STUDY (30 minutes)

Scripture offers examples of each kind of feedback, requested or offered for different purposes.

Let's briefly examine each type.

(1) APPRECIATION

Appreciation helps us feel seen and valued by others. We are often most aware of our need for appreciation in its absence.

Consider the story of Jesus and the lepers, found in Luke 17:11-19. As you listen to a group member read the passage aloud, think about the role that appreciation plays in Jesus' interaction with the lepers.

- Examine Jesus' response in verses 17-18. What is Jesus trying to communicate?

- What purposes do gratitude and praise play in the story?

Appreciation says: "I see you. I understand you. You matter."

- What are other examples in Scripture where God seeks to be seen, understood, or praised?

- In what ways might a desire for appreciation be part of the way that humans are made "in the image of God"? In what ways does our human desire to be seen and valued echo God's desire for our worship and praise? In what way might they be different?

(2) COACHING

Coaching is anything that is aimed at increasing your knowledge or skill. Coaching can include other's suggestions, advice, correction, mentoring, role modeling, or the kind of deep listening and provocative questions that life and career coaches use to facilitate learning.

Jesus spends much of his time on earth coaching – trying to help others better understand God, God's priorities, and how to live, serve and love one another.

Read the disciples request for coaching from Jesus in Luke 11:1.

- As Jews, the disciples presumably have been taught how to pray. Why do they ask Jesus for coaching here?

(3) EVALUATION

Evaluation tells us where we stand vis-à-vis a set of standards or expectations, or each other. Grades, sports competitions, getting that promotion or wanting to know "where this relationship is going" are all examples of the craving and usefulness of evaluation in various areas of our lives.

Yet evaluation is the most emotionally "loud." While we need it to know what we need to work on or what to expect, we also fear it, and we can struggle with experiencing it as judgment of our worthiness for love or respect.

Take a look at what Scripture says about judgment. Have different group members read John 8:2-11 and James 4:11-12 aloud.

- What does Jesus teach the people gathered around him about judgment?

Jesus teaches that God loves each one of us. Read John 3:16-18.

- What do these verses say about God's love for us?

- What does Jesus identify as his current role on earth? What is he *not* on earth to do *at this time*?

12

APPLICATION (30 minutes)

Let's examine how these three types of feedback currently play out in *your* life.

APPRECIATION

- How do you best hear appreciation? Some people need to hear the words "thank you"; others feel appreciated when they feel included, when they are the "go to" person in the group, or through gifts or public recognition. Which forms of appreciation resonate most with you?

- Write down your preferences and then share them with the group. Notice the different ways in which you best receive appreciation.

COACHING

- Name two places in your life where you currently get implicit or explicit coaching that helps you learn and grow.

- Who else might you invite to offer you coaching?

- We will continue to examine the idea of coaching, and coaching people on how to coach you in Session 5.

EVALUATION

Evaluation can be helpful when it helps us understand where we stand, what to work on next, or what to expect.

In Matthew 3:17, Jesus is baptized "And a voice from heaven said, 'This is my Son, whom I love; with him I am well pleased.'" God is communicating his assessment and approval, both to Jesus, and to those around him.

- In what contexts do you find evaluation *helpful* for knowing where you stand and what you need to work on, or to understanding what to expect?

- What kinds of evaluations or judgments do you find most hurtful or upsetting?

- Think of a specific example of a time when you felt judged or evaluated. Do you think the person offering the judgment intended it as evaluation? Was it an (unsuccessful) attempt to offer coaching?

Review your feedback diet from the beginning of this session. Which type(s) of feedback do you want more of, and how might you go about getting it this week?

CLOSING PRAYER

Thank God for His wisdom in providing us with fellowship and the opportunity to learn and grow through our relationship with Him and with others. Ask God to give you insight into the kinds of feedback you need, humility to seek them out, and openness to seeing even off-base or hurtful rebuke as opportunity for growth.

Session 2:

THE CHALLENGES OF
RECEIVING FEEDBACK WELL

To Prepare:
Read TFTF Chapter 1

> **A simple man believes anything – but a prudent man gives thought to his steps.**
>
> **Proverbs 14:15**

INTRODUCTION

We know that feedback is essential for our spiritual growth, as well as our personal and professional growth. We know we're not perfect. We're not omnipotent. We need the perspectives of others to help us see ourselves more clearly and help us improve. We know that we can't forever stay the same.

Yet transformation is hard and sometimes downright painful.

What others say, how they say it, and how closely it seems to strike our core can make us want to throw defiant tantrums shouting, "I'm fine just the way I am! If Jesus accepts me, why can't you?!"

Others' judgments feel unfair. Their suggestions for how to live don't mesh with our own desires, our sense of ourselves, our vision for our lives, or our understanding of scripture. Even appreciation can be challenging. Others praise you – how do you respond with humility? What if you feel it's not deserved?

Daily we can experience the tension between two core human needs:

> The need to learn and grow, and
> The need to be accepted, respected and loved the way we are now.

The needs are consistent with two core Scriptural messages:

> God accepts us just as we are (Romans 5:8), *and*
> We are to be transformed (Romans 12:2).

In this session, we explore what reconciling these two messages might look like in our lives, and how to understand our very human initial reactions to the feedback we get.

GROWING CONNECTED (10 minutes)

Reflect silently for two minutes on the questions below. Then turn to the person next to you and share your thoughts with each other for five minutes.

1. What is a moment in your life where you most clearly experienced God's acceptance?

2. Think of a way in which you have changed – and grown spiritually – in the last few years. When did you first realize you might need to change? What was your initial reaction? How do *you* think about this process of growing, even as God accepts you, all along, the way you are?

Briefly share highlights of this conversation with the group.

STARTERS (20 minutes)

Feedback You Have Found Challenging to Receive

Think of some coaching (advice, suggestions) you have received in the past that you *rejected*. Feedback you didn't take.

Why didn't you take the feedback?

Take 3-5 minutes to discuss as a group your reasons for rejecting the feedback.

Three Triggers

All of the reasons just offered in the group are *good* reasons to reject feedback.

Maybe.

The problem is that we often decide too soon, and based on our initial, triggered reactions to the feedback, what to do with the feedback. All the reasons just given can boil down to three categories of triggered reactions that humans have to feedback:

1) **Truth Triggers** – The substance of the feedback is wrong or not true. It's bad advice, it's under-informed, it's factually "off" in some way, it wouldn't work.

2) **Relationship Triggers** – We react to who the feedback is coming from and how we feel treated by them, or what we think about them. Are they credible? Do we trust them? Do we feel appreciated by them?

3) **Identity Triggers** – the feedback is simply too upsetting, or undermines our sense of self.

Our triggered reactions are understandable. After all, Ecclesiastes 7:5 warns us not to be led astray by the "song of a fool." We need to be discerning about others' advice or judgments – if the advice or input is wrong, certainly we shouldn't take it. However well-respected, upright or faithful others may be, we shouldn't assume their feedback is inherently God speaking to us.

But the *process* of being in relationship with each other *is* God-given, and listening to and wrestling with others' observations and requests is a large part of how we learn and grow as Christians.

The problem is that our initial, triggered reactions themselves can function like noise-canceling headphones, blocking out potentially valuable information. So getting better at receiving feedback, and learning how to grow – personally, professionally, and spiritually – means recognizing our triggered reactions, and better *understanding* the feedback first, before we decide whether to accept it or reject it. It means looking not just for what's wrong with it, but what might also be right about it.

Think about your own feedback experiences. Which of the triggered reactions (truth, relationship, identity) do you think you experience most often? Which resonates most with you right now?

BIBLE STUDY (30 minutes)

Part I: God's Willingness to Listen

Have a group member read Numbers 11:10-16 aloud. Moses and the Israelites are in the wilderness, eating the manna from heaven daily, and the people are starting to complain to Moses about the tedium of the diet. As you listen to the conversation between Moses and God, notice:

- How does Moses talk to God? If his comments were directed at you, how would you be tempted to respond? How is Moses feeling? How might God feel?
- How does God respond?

Part II: Responding in the Moment

Invite three people to read aloud the verses below.

- Proverbs 15:1
- Proverbs 15:5
- Proverbs 15:22

What implications do these verses have for how we respond in the moment to feedback?

In what ways do you find these verses challenging?

Part III: The Nature of Growth

Jesus uses many metaphors to help us understand the process of growth and maturity. Consider what Jesus says about the work of the Father as gardener. Read John 15:1-4.

Notice that we as Christians may need to be pruned or "cut back" sometimes in order to be more fruitful. In this sense, coaching is an opportunity to cut away habits or behavior or attitudes that hurt others, or inhibit our own growth elsewhere.

- In what ways might God be pruning you today?

- What impact does the fact that we are "already clean" (v3) have on your ability to and experience of receiving feedback?

- Based on verse 4, what is your responsibility to do in the pruning process?

APPLICATION (20 minutes)

- What is a current piece of feedback, or area of your life, where you feel the nudge to either let go (of a hurtful attitude, behavior, or set of feelings) or to grow (to add practices or try something new)?

- What might help you invite feedback this week and/or respond more positively to it? What practical tips do you have for yourself for what to do in the moment?

CLOSING PRAYER

Ask God to give you the curiosity to understand what others are trying to say to you, the humility see them as valuable partners in your journey, and the confidence and self-acceptance of who you are in Christ.

Session 3:

THE CHALLENGE TO SEE WHAT THE GIVER MEANS

To Prepare:
Read TFTF Chapter 3

**The purposes of a person's heart are deep waters,
but one who has insight draws them out.**

Proverbs 20:5

INTRODUCTION

One of the most challenging things about feedback is that it usually arrives in the form of vague, sweeping labels:

"You need to be more proactive."

"I don't think you're following God's will." or

"Your kids need more discipline."

More discipline? Which kind? Which kid? Do you mean that you think I'm not disciplining them at all, or that my attempts are ineffective? What exactly are you recommending? How is it that you know so much about raising kids when you've never had any yourself? (Just curious).

These reactions assume that the feedback you get is clear and direct to begin with. So often it is instead indirect, implied, or inferred. Why wasn't I asked to join the new committee? Why didn't anyone say anything to me after my presentation? Why didn't you respond to my email?

Are you trying to tell me something? And if so, what? In this session we explore how we might be able to both hear and understand the feedback we're receiving.

GROWING CONNECTED (10 minutes)

Think about someone you find difficult. It might be a co-worker, boss, customer, friend, family member, or fellow group member. Without revealing the person's identity, complete one of the following sentences and share your "label" with the group.

    a. *He's just too* _____.

    b. *I wish she were just a little less* _____.

    c. *Why can't he be more* _____?

    d. *It would be so helpful if she could just* _____.

When we describe what's "wrong" with someone else, we use labels ourselves. They are shorthand for a host of annoying habits, upsetting behavior, or unfulfilled expectations that we have in our interactions with them. To us, these labels come with a highlight (or "lowlight") movie reel attached. The problem is that when we're on the receiving end, the highlight movie reel isn't attached.

Go around the room again and share the kinds of labels that you have heard as feedback from someone in your own life at some stage. Examples:
> *"You shouldn't take yourself so seriously."*
> *"You angst too much – you should be more decisive!"*
> *"You need to speak up more."*
> *"You need to get a handle on your temper."*
> *"You'd find someone if you weren't so picky."*

Also share what you found frustrating about the label you received.

BIBLE STUDY (35 minutes)

<u>Part I</u>: Wrong Spotting

Focusing on what's wrong with a situation or with the feedback compromises our ability to learn from the moment. Read the following passages.

- Mark 2:1-7
- Mark 2:23-28
- Mark 3:1-6

What are the things that the Pharisees find wrong with Jesus and his disciples?

What are the Pharisees missing out on in focusing on what's wrong?

<u>Part II</u>: Unpacking Labels

The other challenge to receiving feedback is whether we understand what others are saying. To understand Jesus' teaching, we need to look backward as to the context and basis for his conclusions, and to look forward as to what it means for the listener and for us. Read Mark 10:35-45 with both those lenses.

- When James and John come to Jesus, what would you say they are looking for?

- What is the response that Jesus offers to them?

- What does Jesus draw upon to support his conclusion (looking backward)?

- Where is his advice going to? What implications does it have for James and John? What implications does it have for us?

APPLICATION (40 minutes)

First, understand.
Instead of deciding right away whether a piece of feedback is right or wrong, we need to more deeply understand it. As described on page 57 of TFTF, we can better understand what the feedback means by

(1) looking backward and thinking about what the person who gave the feedback might have *noticed, expected, or felt that led them to give the feedback*. Or

(2) looking forward and wondering: *If I were going to take this coaching, what exactly does the giver want me to do differently?*

Individually, choose a piece of feedback you have received from someone, or feedback you sense you are getting from God – that He is nudging you to change your behavior or thinking or attitude on some front. Write down the "label" in the middle, and see if you can identify where the feedback might be coming from and going to. (5 minutes).

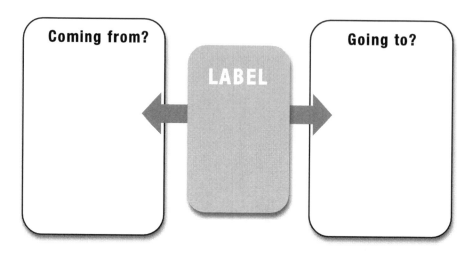

In pairs, share the feedback that you were just analyzing. What did you learn when you thought about where the feedback might be coming from, or where it might be going in terms of what changes the feedback giver is asking you to consider? (10 minutes).

As a group. What surprised you about this process? What did you learn that is new, or gives you something to think about?

Second, figure out what might be right.
In TFTF the authors point out that we are extremely good at wrong-spotting – figuring out what is wrong with the feedback we're given. The problem is that we will *always* be able to find something wrong with the feedback. But that doesn't mean that there isn't also something that might be right about it, and might warrant some further thought and prayer.

Take your own example of frustrating feedback you shared at the beginning of this session. Sort through the feedback by using the boxes below to acknowledge what you feel is wrong with the feedback. But don't stop there. Also ask yourself the questions – what might be right about the feedback? In what ways might this feedback be valuable to me?

What's wrong
with the feedback?

What might be right
about the feedback?

If you wanted to better understand a piece of coaching that someone in your life has for you, how might you have a follow-up conversation?

CLOSING PRAYER

Ask God to help you this week to manage your triggered reactions to feedback you receive, and to be curious to first learn more about what your giver means.

Session 4:

THE CHALLENGE TO
SEE YOURSELF CLEARLY

....

To Prepare:
Read TFTF Chapter 4

....

Who can discern his errors? Forgive my hidden faults.

Psalm 19:12

INTRODUCTION

Part of what is hard about receiving feedback is that it is difficult to see ourselves clearly. We are very aware of our own intentions, but rarely of the impact our words and behavior have on others.

In an effort to make our friend feel less anxious before a big meeting, we reassured them they had nothing to worry about – they would do fine! Instead of feeling reassured, they felt dismissed, unheard, and like we don't really understand what they are going through. We meant to be supportive. We came off as clueless, or worse, callous.

Without each other, we have only our own biased and incomplete impressions of ourselves. We remain blind to how we impact others, how others see (or don't see) Christ in and through us. If we are to be imitators and ambassadors of Christ, we need each other in order to see ourselves – how we show up, how we're perceived, how we're impacting others, whether and how we're representing Christ – more clearly.

GROWING CONNECTED (10 minutes)

Have you ever watched yourself on videotape, or listened to yourself on audiotape? Have you ever had a friend point out a habit you have, or pattern to your behavior that you were completely unaware of?

While we can see ourselves in the mirror, we can't see ourselves in motion, in life. The following things often land in a blind spot for all of us:

Body language
Facial expressions
Tone of voice
Patterns of behavior
Our impact on others & their resulting perceptions of us

What kinds of things have you been surprised to learn about yourself?

STARTERS (30 minutes)

Think of a piece of feedback you have received from someone (or many someones) that has struck you as "wrong" or simply baffling because it is so mis-aligned with who you know you are. Perhaps one of the following resonates for you:

They said you were	When you know you are
Aloof	Shy
Intimidating	Direct
Elitist	Someone with high standards
Overbearing	An extrovert
Oversensitive	Sensitive
Insensitive	Honest
Bossy	Assertive

If comfortable, share the ~~accusation~~ feedback you got with the group, and how it made you feel.

Individually, use the lens of the Gap Map (TFTF pages 78-79) to try to better understand where the feedback might have been coming from.

Start on the right by writing down the upsetting feedback you got, then jump to the middle to try to identify the behavior ("My behavior") that prompted the feedback. Now you can work backwards in time to think about your intentions behind the behavior ("My intentions") and the thoughts and feelings that led to those intentions ("My thoughts and feelings"). Finally, work forward from the behavior to imagine the impact it had on the other person ("The impact on them") and their resulting story about you.

> *Example:* Julie got feedback that she was intimidating. Thinking back, she wondered whether the behavior the feedback giver might have observed was her talking for most of the meeting and answering all the questions that came up. It was a topic she was particularly passionate and knowledgeable about, so she wanted to be sure to share her thoughts with the group. In retrospect, talking so much without inviting others into the conversation might have had the unintended impact on others of shutting them down, such that they are telling a story about how she's intimidating.

Jot down notes to yourself below (7 minutes).

In pairs, share your chart and insights with your partner, and learn about theirs. (13 minutes).

- What insights did you have in this process?

- What do you want to re-think or work to change? (For instance: I've been described as aloof, and realize that the fact that I feel awkward might actually be making others feel awkward, when I don't say hello or make eye contact in the hallways. I want to try to....)

As a group, what surprised you about this process?

How might you go about getting more information from others, or experiment with making a change in your behavior, on this front?

BIBLE STUDY (20 minutes)

Part I: Honest Mirrors

Examine the following verses:

- Proverbs 26:28

- Proverbs 27:5-6

- Proverbs 12:15

What implications do these verses have for who gives us feedback and how they do it?

Part II: Sharing Observations

Have someone read Matthew 18:15 aloud.

- Why do we need others to show us our shortcomings, mistakes, or unintended hurtful behavior?

- How are we to share these faults with each other?

Part III: Our Stance

Read Romans 12:3.

- What implications does thinking of yourself with "sober judgment" have for giving feedback? For receiving feedback?

APPLICATION (30 minutes)

Re-read or skim pages 93-94 of TFTF describing honest mirrors and supportive mirrors. Then have someone read the following aloud:

> A **supportive mirror** shows us at our best, on a good day, under flattering light. We need supportive mirrors to reassure us that the mistakes we made, the behavior we are ashamed of, or criticism we just received, are not the sum total of who we are. A supportive mirror shows us as God sees us – as his beloved child, made in his image.

> An **honest mirror** shows us how we look – right now – when we're not at our best, and there is something for us to work on. It can show us something we need to see in order to grow, even if that something is painful.

Discuss the following questions: When you get upsetting feedback, what role are you usually asking those in your community to play?

- In what instances are you asking simply for support and reassurance – to gain perspective or commiserate about what's *wrong* with the feedback (why it's not true, not relevant, or not your fault)?

- At what point do you tend to feel ready to invite others to be an honest mirror to help you see what might be *right* about the feedback?

- How might we tap each other – in fellowship – to provide both supportive mirrors and honest mirrors?

- What would you like to know about others (or about their opinion of you) that would make it easier to hear what they are saying as an "honest mirror"?

CLOSING PRAYER

Thank God for His eternal acceptance of and love for us, even as we struggle to hear how others might perceive us. Ask God to reveal the things we need to see about ourselves, and our impact on others, so that others may see and experience His love through us.

Session 5

THE CHALLENGE OF BEING ME
Understanding Your Unique, God-Given Profile

To Prepare:
Read TFTF Chapters 7 & 8

For you created my inmost being; you knit me together in my mother's womb. I praise you because I am fearfully and wonderfully made; your works are wonderful, I know that full well.

Psalm 139:13-14

INTRODUCTION

God's creation includes seemingly infinite variety, not just across the flora, fish and furry or flying creatures, but even within the human race. Each of us is unique, knit together by God – fearfully and wonderfully -- in our mother's womb.

While we have been fully known by God since before birth, understanding ourselves – our gifts and our challenges – is a life-long journey.

Our uniqueness extends to how we experience feedback. Some of us are highly emotionally sensitive, so that just a whisper of disappointment can be devastating. Others of us are quite emotionally even-keel; even a harsh dressing down is experienced as momentarily disappointing. How far you swing emotionally in the wake of positive or negative feedback, and how long it takes you to recover, differs dramatically from person to person.

Having greater understanding to our own feedback profile enables us to coach those around us in *how* to best offer us coaching, so that we can hear it and learn from it. And understanding each other in any team or community strengthens our ability to learn and grow together.

GROWING CONNECTED (12 minutes)

Invite people to talk in pairs about the following:

Choose a particular context – your work team, a friendship, your significant other or with your children. Do you suspect you are on the more sensitive or less sensitive end of the spectrum in this group? How does your relative sensitivity influence these relationships, and how (or whether) you offer each other feedback?

> *Example*: I think I'm more sensitive to feedback than my sister is. She seems unfazed by the world's feedback to her. She offers me plenty of direct – sometimes harsh – feedback. I rarely offer her feedback because I know it would hurt my feelings if it were said to me. Though I'm not sure she would actually be upset by it!

STARTERS (18 Minutes)

- **2-minute takeaway:** What struck you most about the chapters you read in preparation for this session, or the conversation that you just had about your own profile?

- **Positive feedback.** Let's imagine you receive a bit of positive feedback in this relationship. How much does this impact your mood? How long does that bump in mood last? All morning? All day? All week? What implications does this have for how much you care about positive feedback?

- **Negative feedback.** Let's imagine you receive a bit of negative feedback in this same context – a complaint, criticism, judgment, or helpful "suggestion" that doesn't feel so helpful. How much does this influence your mood, and how long does it take you to recover? All morning? All day? All year? What implications does this have for how you handle the feedback you get in that relationship? Do you avoid it? Dismiss it? Feel devastated by it?

- **Different sensitivity.** Some of us are more sensitive to feedback than others. Discuss as pairs the following questions and then report out to the group.

What are the advantages of being sensitive?

What are the challenges of being sensitive?

What are the advantages of being more even-keeled?

What are the challenges of being more even-keeled?

BIBLE STUDY (30 Minutes)

<u>Part I</u>: Our Individual Responses

Joseph's brothers sold him into slavery, something he could have been bitter about. Read Genesis 45:1-15 and notice Joseph's reactions to how things have unfolded.

- How does Joseph respond to the knowledge that it is now his brothers who are in need?

- Reread verses 5-7. What is the reasoning Joseph attributes to what has happened?

- What impact does this reasoning have on his ability to move forward in relationship with his brothers?

<u>Part II</u>: Our Approaches to Others

Jesus approached conversations with groups of people quite differently. Have different group members read aloud the passages below. As you listen, compare and contrast Jesus' approaches to the situations.

- Matthew 21:12-17
- John 12:1-8

As a group, discuss the following questions:

- How would you describe Jesus' tone and approach in the two passages above?

46

- What is the message Jesus is trying to communicate in each scenario? How does his approach align with his message and audience?

Read Matthew 7:6.

- If others have wisdom to share with you, how can they present it in a way that you will hear it as a pearl?

APPLICATION (30 Minutes)

What do you notice about your own wiring?

- In what ways does your sensitivity vary depending on the context (work/home) or the relationship (strangers/friends)?

- How does your own profile (sensitivity) affect how you *give* feedback to others? Do you see differences in sensitivity showing up in particular relationships in your life?

Looking back at your reflections from this session, how would you coach your coaches on how to give you feedback? If you were to create an "operating manual" for how others can best give you feedback given your particular wiring and preferences, what instructions would you include? The key question is – how can you help others understand how you best receive feedback so they can best help you grow?

Take 15 minutes to journal your answers to the questions below to start developing a "Guide to Giving Me Feedback" that you can share with others. Note: you, and your preferences for receiving feedback will likely continue to evolve. Your reflections below are merely a snapshot of your current understanding of yourself, to be revised as you discover what works best in practice.

- Where, when, and how would you (ideally) like feedback to be offered?

- How do you like to be appreciated? If someone wanted to celebrate or recognize you, what should they do? What should they *not* do?

- How do you best receive coaching? If someone had advice for you, how would you suggest they share it with you?

- What pet-peeves do you have about feedback?

- How sensitive are you to feedback? How high or low do you "swing"? How long does it take you to recover?

- What are you currently working on? *Not* working on?

As a next step, who might you share these preferences with in the next week to help them give you feedback more effectively? A spouse? Co-worker? Team? Friend?

Invite them to answer the questions as well, and discuss together. In doing so, you can deepen these relationships, ease their challenges, and begin to collaborate (even) more effectively.

CLOSING PRAYER

Take a few minutes to thank God for the richness and variety of humanity in the world. Pray for greater awareness and acceptance of how you are uniquely created, wisdom on how to communicate in light of differences, and audacity to invite others into your journey.

Session 6:

THE CHALLENGE OF WE
Relationship Systems and Being in Fellowship

To Prepare:
Read TFTF Chapter 6

You hypocrite, first take the log out of your own eye, and then you will see clearly to take the speck out of your brother's eye.

Matthew 7:4-5

INTRODUCTION

Throughout the New Testament we are exhorted to live our lives "in fellowship" with others, as well as in fellowship with God. Yet we often have a bigger reaction to *who* is giving us the feedback than we do to what they are saying.

Living in fellowship is hard. Other people don't treat us the way we think we deserve to be treated. They don't love us the way God does. They are difficult themselves, and then they have the nerve to point out *our* faults and shortcomings.

If we want to understand the feedback we have for each other, we have to take on the deeply interactive nature of our human relationships. Understanding the feedback we have for each other on our teams, in our friendships, in our congregations and in our marriages, often means that the unit of analysis isn't just you. Or just me. It's often you+me. Or you+me+our kids, colleagues, or friends.

We are all reacting to each other, and it's the friction in the interaction between us that is *creating* the feedback we have for each other. You want me to be less bossy. But I'm bossy because you're so passive. You say you're passive because I'm bossy. Who is the one who needs to change?

In this regard, we need to see others – especially those we experience as difficult – as the way we are most likely to learn about ourselves and about grace. These relationships are the greenhouses where God can and does grow us.

God created each of us as unique, and as such, every pairing has unique ways in which we bump up against each other, and unique ways we can support, honor, and help each other grow. And sometimes that growth comes from the most surprising people.

GROWING CONNECTED (15 minutes)

Invite people to talk in pairs about the following:

- What particularly resonated for you about Chapters 5 & 6?

- Share an example of feedback you have received in the past, where you have had a bigger reaction to *who* gave you the feedback, than you did to the feedback itself. What tripped the relationship trigger? Was it what you thought about them (not credible, not trustworthy?) or how you felt treated by them (not appreciated, not accepted, no autonomy?)?

Discuss in pairs, and then in the group, share a two-minute takeaway from your discussion.

STARTERS (25 minutes)

Choose a current relationship with friction – chances are someone wants you to change, or you wish they would change. Journal about the following questions before discussing.

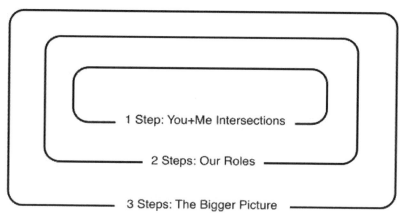

Other players, processes, policies, physical environment

- STEP 1 - What are some of the individual differences between you and the other person that create some difficulty? Differences in preferences, work styles, risk tolerance, anxiety, tasks you find rewarding or stressful, implicit rules about relationships or the way things "should be"?

    - *Examples:* I'm a saver and she's a spender; I'm detail-oriented and he's big picture; I assume friends are in touch with each other at least every few days, while she assumes we just pick up the conversation where we left off, even after several months' silence.

    Why might God create these kinds of differences, and in what ways might they be complementary?

- STEP 2 – What roles do you two currently play that may exacerbate the challenge?
    - *Examples:* These can be formal roles (like peers who share responsibility, or boss-employee, or older-younger sibling) or informal roles (I'm the one who takes initiative to do the planning; you're the one who tracks the finances and pays the bills; you're the one who always plays devil's advocate).

- STEP 3 - Taking one more step back, what other factors – people, geography, physical setup, policies, or other outside influences – exacerbate the challenge between you?
  - *Examples:* The geographical distance and time zones make it difficult for us to connect; the fact that you are available during the day means mom always calls you first; the new work flow process means you don't hear about problems until late in the game.

BIBLE STUDY (30 minutes)

Part I: Why Context Matters

Sometimes we can't hear the messages because of who the messenger is and the context we're in. Read Luke 4:14-30.

- What impact does being in Nazareth, the city where Jesus was brought up, have on the ability of people to hear his message?

- Why is it that "no prophet is accepted in his hometown"?

- Why would the people in the synagogue be furious (v28)?

- At the beginning of the session you thought about a time when you had a bigger reaction to the person giving you the advice than you did to the advice itself. In what ways was your experience similar or different from Jesus's experience here?

Part II: Loving Others

Our relationship exists both with God and with others. Read Matthew 22:36-40 and discuss the questions below.

- What is the relationship between these two commandments?

- In what ways have you been challenged to love your neighbor as yourself?

- To what extent do you find that it's the feedback you have for *yourself* sometimes that is the most painful? How does the struggle to accept and love yourself influence how you also judge others?

Part III: Feedback for Each Other

Being in fellowship with one another is challenging. Read Matthew 7:4-5 aloud.

- Why is it so much easier to focus on the "speck" in someone else's eye?

- What is the "log" currently in your own eye?

APPLICATION (20 minutes)

On TFTF page 110, the authors suggest that people who you like the least, and who are least like you, can sometimes be the most valuable players in our learning.

- In what ways have you found this to be true in your own life?

- Who in your life do you currently find challenging to interact with?

- How might they be an unsuspectingly rich resource for your learning?

Return to thinking about the relationship with friction that you were analyzing earlier in the session (3 Steps Back).

- What might you learn from this relationship?

- How might you change the way you interact with or perceive the person in light of this insight?

CLOSING PRAYER

Thank God for the opportunity to live in relationship with Him and with others, and for His sovereignty over relationships and situations that seem daunting and unmanageable to us. Ask Him to help you to see and hear wisdom in others' feedback, even when delivered by the unlikeliest of messengers.

SESSION 7

Boundaries, Rest and Honoring Healthy Relationships

....

To Prepare:
Read TFTF Chapter 10

....

I care very little if I am judged by you or by any human court; indeed, I do not even judge myself.

1 Corinthians 4:3

INTRODUCTION

Is it okay to turn down feedback? To say that you don't even want to hear it?

Yes.

Being able to establish limits on the feedback you get – when, where, how, by whom, and about what – is essential. You may be in a relationship filled with unrelenting criticism and judgment. As you transition into a new role – becoming a spouse, evolving as a parent, taking on a new position at work – you may need space and time to sort out how *you* want to handle this new role, so you need space rather than suggestions. You may simply be overwhelmed with all the things you are already working on, and more advice isn't helpful right now.

In these moments, boundaries are essential to your well-being, and the well-being of your relationships. Pressure that can come from criticism, advice, or even "helpful" but unsolicited suggestions builds resentment, strains relationships, and ultimately inhibits rather than helps your ability to self-reflect and grow.

If you can't say "no" to feedback, your "yes's" are not freely given.

GROWING CONNECTED (10 minutes)

"Boundaries" describe your ability to manage others' access to your emotional well-being. This includes letting people know that you aren't taking their coaching, or accepting their assessment as fair. It also can mean letting people know that you need them to keep their suggestions or judgments to themselves.

1. When have you experienced a need for boundaries when it comes to feedback?

2. Why can it be hard to create boundaries when it comes to others giving you feedback? If you draw boundaries, what do you fear? From others? From God?

STARTERS (15 minutes)

Examine the three boundaries discussed on pages 210-212 of TFTF. What are instances where you have wanted to say any of the following to someone giving you feedback?

1) I may not take your advice.
2) I don't want feedback about that subject, not right now.
3) Stop, or I will leave the relationship.

In that instance, did you share the thought with the other person? Why or why not?

Part of what is challenging about feedback and boundaries is deciding: Should I try taking their advice? Should I talk to them about keeping their opinions to themselves? There are many reasons you may decide not to take advice, at least not right now.

Discuss as a group. How do *you* decide whether the boundary is healthy and needed, or whether it's a rationalization for dismissing hard truths or good insights?

BIBLE STUDY (35 minutes)

<u>Part I</u>: Better Not to Listen

Invite a group member to read Genesis 3:1-7. *If* we think of the serpent as offering advice or instruction to Eve, what are the attributes of the advice? As you listen, pay attention to what is tempting or "true" about what the serpent says.

- Why does Eve (and then Adam) take the serpent's advice? What about it is tempting?

- When have you received advice that was tempting, and perhaps had elements of truth embedded in it, yet was wrong or problematic for larger reasons?

    Feel free to share with the group, including what tipped you off to a problem, and what helped you make a decision about whether to follow the advice.

<u>Part II</u>: Nonconformity to the Norm

Following Christ necessitates resisting the pressures of the society around us. Read Matthew 10:16-22

- What are the disciples up against as they are sent out?

- What does Jesus ask of them in verse 22? What implications does this have for us as we navigate the ocean of opinions and advice in this world?

Close relationships are important – and can require boundaries to be in line with Christ. Read Matthew 12:46-50.

- How does Jesus' definition of family differ from the mainstream understanding at the time?

- What does this mean for how we relate to the people in our lives?

APPLICATION (30 minutes)

Often we feel pressure to take feedback, even if there are more important things we need to work on, or we're not sure the assessment is fair. We worry about what others will think of us. We fear they will take our rejection of their feedback as a rejection of *them.*

Yet, letting our yes be yes and our no be no (James 5:12) means being able to say "yes" to some feedback and "no" to others.

- Is there a boundary that you would like to draw when it comes to feedback? This could be a boundary with someone else in your life, or it could be one with yourself.

- Why does a boundary feel important to draw here?

- How might you share the desire for that boundary with the other person (or with yourself)?

    a) What impact is their behavior having on you?

    b) What dilemma do you experience in trying to draw the boundary?

    c) What specifically would you like them to start or stop doing? On what time frame?

d) What are the consequences if they can't keep their judgments and advice to themselves? *Remember: your purpose isn't to make a threat; it's to issue clear warning. They need to know the consequences in order to make an informed decision as to whether to accept your request.*

CLOSING PRAYER

Ask God for wisdom to discern wise from foolish counsel, and for courage to have the conversations you need to have. Pray that He touch others' hearts so that they can hear our hurt, our need, and our true intentions.

Session 8

Embracing the Growth Identity God Gave You

....

To Prepare:
Read TFTF Chapter 9

....

**Therefore, if anyone is in Christ, he is a new creation.
The old has passed away; behold, the new has come.**

2 Corinthians 5:17

INTRODUCTION

Change is key to the Gospel message. Because of his great love for us, God made us alive with Christ even when we were dead in transgressions (Ephesians 2:1, 4-5).

Given this, we can't help but be changed by our relationship with Christ. If we are in Christ, we are a new creation. The old has passed, and the new has come.

Yet so often we feel stuck. If I'm supposed to be a new creation, why am I still fixed in my old ways? Why do I still get frustrated with my kids? Why do I still snap at my spouse when they are trying to be helpful? Why do I still struggle to like my neighbor and have trouble managing my doubts? I've tried everything. Nothing has changed. I'm going to be this way forever.

The stories we tell ourselves about who we are, and what we are capable of, have a profound impact on our reaction to challenge and on our ability to change and grow. Here we explore ways to make ourselves fertile soil for change, being open to how God might want to work in and through us. We also examine how we measure growth and success in the Christian life.

The good news is that we are not the main change agents in this process of transformation. We are not changing simply by our own strength, determination or will power. We can change. We do change. Even if we don't want to – we *will* be changed.

GROWING CONNECTED (15 minutes)

Identity is the story we tell ourselves about ourselves – what we're like, what we stand for, what we're good at, what we're capable of.

Invite people to talk in pairs about the following:

1. If you had 3 minutes to tell someone who you are, what would you tell them? What would you want them to know about you?

2. What is a situation you found challenging in the moment? What did you learn from it afterwards?

3. What do you find yourself using to measure your success in life?

STARTERS (10 minutes)

- **2-minute takeaway:** What struck you most about the chapter you read in preparation for this session (Chapter 9 on Growth Identity)?

  What do you notice about what you chose to share in introducing yourself to someone?

- **Fixed or Growth Mindset:** Do you think you tend toward having a fixed or a growth mindset? Has this changed over time? Does it shift depending on the context (for example: you have a growth mindset as to your exercise regime or parenting journey, but a fixed mindset when it comes to your relationship with your step-brother)?

BIBLE STUDY (40 minutes)

Part I: The Context in Which We Live

Have a group member read Ephesians 1:3-14 aloud. Notice the following:

- God chose *you* in him before the creation of the world to be holy and blameless in his sight (v4).
- In him we have redemption through his blood, the forgiveness of sins – which he lavished on us with all wisdom and understanding (v7-8).

In what ways is the Christian journey of growth different than the secular context?

Reread the passage.

Write below the action verbs of what God is doing:

What are the consequences for us because of the choices God has made?

Part II: The Driving Force

Invite four people to read aloud each of the verses below. As you listen, reflect on the role that *you* play in change:

- Ezekiel 36:26
- Ephesians 2:22
- Philippians 1:6
- Ephesians 4:22-24

What role does God play in your change and transformation?

What role do you play in your own change and transformation?

Part III: Our Stance

Have someone paraphrase the concept of the second score from page 202-204 of TFTF. Then read the story of the rich man with two sons in Luke 15:11-32.

- What is your reaction to the actions of the younger brother? (v11-16)

- Examine the behaviors of the younger brother (v17-21). What second score would you give the younger brother?

- The older brother remains dutifully with the father. How would you describe his life choices?

- Focus on verses 28-30. What second score would you give the older brother?

APPLICATION (25 minutes)

The chapter on moving from a fixed to a growth identity points out that particularly when we are stuck in a fixed mindset ("I am who I am. I'm not going to change.") we can be particularly prone to hearing feedback as evaluation or judgment. Three ways to nudge ourselves toward a growth mindset are to (1) sort toward coaching (2) give yourself a second score and (3) recognize our own journey of transformation.

1) *Sort Toward Coaching*

In what ways do you currently feel evaluated or judged?

What advice or coaching might be hidden within the evaluation? What is the judgment, rating or ranking "telling" you that you might want to work on?

What aspects of this advice might you want to experiment with? What coaching do you have for yourself here?

Remember: you get to decide whether you want to take the coaching and make the changes others are suggesting. Before you decide whether to accept or reject the feedback, figure out what of it *might* be helpful to you.

2) *Give Yourself a Second Score*

Describe the last disappointment or frustration you faced.

On a scale of 1-10, with 1 being "catastrophic failure" and 10 being "unmitigated success", how would you rate the situation?

On the same scale, how would you rate your own response to the situation?

Given all the dimensions you've discussed during these sessions, what will you do differently to expedite your own learning?

3) *Recognize Your Own Journey of Transformation*

Remember your 7 or 17 or 37-year-old self. In what ways is the current version of you different from who you were then?

In what ways do you hope the version of yourself 7 years from now will be different from how are you now?

CLOSING PRAYER

Thank God that He loves us as we are and that we are not stuck as we are. Ask that the Holy Spirit continue to transform you to be more and more like Jesus. Amen.

LEADER'S GUIDE

LEADER'S GUIDE

This study is intended to equip individuals to skillfully invite and fruitfully wrestle with feedback from others in order accelerate their growth - personally, professionally, and spiritually. Alongside that, this study creates small groups who are better equipped, after eight weeks of candid discussion about the challenges and responsibility to learn and change, to help each other grow in more open, honest, and earnest ways.

As a community, you might consider keeping these groups intact for future discussion and study, creating the opportunity to tackle a next topic or book together, and to capitalize on the group's new skills and understanding of each other to spur individual and collective growth.

Leader Notes on Individual Sessions:

Before you lead this study we recommend you read *Thanks for the Feedback* (TFTF) in full and read through all of the sessions, so you know what is ahead, and can make connections and answer questions when they come up.

Below we provide a summary of key concepts and purposes for each session, and tips that will help you guide the group.

Depending on the size of the group, and the interest in the weekly topic, the sessions may run between 60 and 90 minutes. A lively group can dig in and spend more than 2 hours if you would like to spend more time on each section of the discussion. Set expectations up front so that people know if you are going to pace yourselves differently from the suggesting timing.

As you facilitate discussion, you will develop insights and suggestions of your own for improving this Bible Study and Workbook. Please share these suggestions with us, so that we can incorporate your coaching into later editions of this guide, and allow others to benefit from your experience.

You can send your observations, anything that you found helpful, and suggestions for improvement to us at feedback@speckbooks.com.

Session 1: Introduction & What Is Feedback?

You may want to schedule slightly more time for this session (up to 2 hours) since introductions, discussing group ground rules, and getting used to the structure of the study often takes a bit of additional time. Once the group gets the rhythm of the sessions, and grabs hold of the content, they will come prepared, and sessions will tend to run more efficiently.

Main Messages

1. Feedback in all areas of our lives is an opportunity to learn and grow in two ways:
   a. How we handle the feedback we get from others is an opportunity to demonstrate graciousness and humility, and a chance to strengthen relationships, rather than allow them to fracture.
   b. God speaks to us in many ways, including using messengers we might least expect, and methods we might not instantly recognize.
2. In order to learn and grow, we need 3 kinds of feedback: Appreciation, Coaching, and Evaluation.
   a. Group members have an opportunity to reflect on their own current "feedback diet" in some area of their life, and to think about what they might like more of, and how to get it.
   b. Examples of each type of feedback can be found in the Scriptures, and offers us deeper understanding of the nature and purpose of appreciation, coaching, and evaluation on our spiritual journey.

Tips for facilitating Session 1
   - The first session is a great time to establish both explicit and implicit group norms, and set the tone for self-reflection, honesty, and kindness toward ourselves and others.
   - Be sure to include everyone in the group discussion; take advantage of the numerous scripture readings in this session to invite quieter members of the group to read one of them aloud.
   - You should think about the discussion questions yourself ahead of time so you can offer thoughts for yourself if the group seems stalled, or needs an example in order to better understand the question. For instance, "Think of two or three examples of coaching you are currently getting in your life" might prompt you to offer:
     o "I'm in a new role at my job, and working hard to try to figure out what is needed. I'm getting lots of "advice" from peers, but I'm not sure it's on target," or
     o "I'm learning how to parent a defiant toddler/teenager (or cope with an empty nest), and I find that I'm going to a particular friend frequently for suggestions and perspective" or

o "I'm being challenged to find a way to deal with my resentment, and I've been doing a lot of reading and praying for guidance."

Your openness and honesty will help signal others that this is a safe space to share their struggle.

Session 2: Challenges of Receiving Feedback Well

Be sure to read Chapter 1 of TFTF, think about your own triggered reactions to feedback, and about ways in which God may be pruning you, or nudging you to change right now. How do you experience the dual messages in the Scriptures that God accepts you as you are, and also challenges us to change and grow?

Main Messages
1. One of the central challenges of feedback is that it sits at the junction of two human needs: the need to learn and grow, and the need to be accepted, respected, and loved the way we are now. This message is echoed in the Scriptures as God demonstrates full acceptance and love of each of us as His children, while simultaneously inviting us to repent, be transformed, and continue to learn and grow in our relationship with him.
2. Human beings have natural and predictable triggered reactions to the feedback we get, and understanding these triggers can help us refrain from "wrong-spotting" and rejecting input from others. Our triggered reactions prompt us to "wrong-spot" and throw out feedback too soon; the wise listen for what's right about the feedback, rather than simply what's wrong.

Session 3: Challenge to SEE What the Giver Means

Read Chapter 3 of TFTF and think about examples of vague, label-filled feedback that you have given, and that you have gotten, in your life. Fill out the chart that asks you to unpack a label by thinking about where it is coming from, and where it is going to, before the session so that you can answer questions about how to do it from the group.

Main Messages

1. Jesus spends a significant amount of time clarifying what He means when he is coaching us – teaching us – what it means to follow Him. In our conversations we should seek the same level of clarity of understanding before we decide what we want to do with the feedback.

2. Feedback often arrives in vague "labels" – like "be more pro-active," "be more confident," or "be more considerate." We often assume we know what the giver means, and jump to wrong-spotting in order to dismiss the feedback. Instead we need to more fully understand what the giver is trying to tell us, and we can do that by:

   a) Looking backward to where the feedback is coming from, or forward to what, specifically, the giver is suggesting that we change.

   b) Acknowledging what we find wrong about the feedback AND asking what might be "right" about the feedback.

Session 4: Challenge to SEE Yourself Clearly

Read chapter 4 of TFTF, paying particular attention to the Gap Map (p. 78-79) and Honest and Supportive Mirrors (p. 93-94). Think about an example of something you discovered about yourself that you were previously unaware of. This might have come from watching yourself on videotape, or some tough feedback you got that gave you sudden insight into how you were being perceived. Be ready to share this with the group, and to answer questions about how to fill out their Gap Map.

Main Messages

1. One of the challenges of feedback is how difficult it is to see ourselves accurately. Our own facial expressions, tone of voice, verbal habits, behavior, and the impact we have on others are all invisible to us. We need others in order to see ourselves clearly. We often get feedback that is baffling or seems "wrong" because it's out of sync with our sense of ourselves.

2. Jesus and the early Christians were very aware of the extent to which they needed each other in order to develop the church and remain on the true path. Paul and others exhort us to go to each other in love and in Fellowship to help each other see the need to learn and grow spiritually.

Session 5: Challenge of Being ME

God's creation includes is a wide range of emotional sensitivity to feedback among human beings, including the human beings in your small group. As a leader, notice the differences in wiring amongst the people in the room. The group itself is a live study for the challenge of people interacting with one another given their different wiring.

Before leading this session, read the relevant chapters in TFTF and think about your own profile. Consider some examples of differences in profile in some of your most important relationships. Be prepared to share these to stimulate conversation, if needed.

Main Messages

1. Understanding yourself, and the ways in which you are different from others, helps us to manage our own reactions to feedback.

2. Living in fellowship means being thoughtful about the ways in which differences in sensitivity to feedback affect how we appreciate each other, coach each other, and learn from each other. The community benefits from this variety, even as we need to be mindful of it.

3. The person best placed to coach others on how to offer you feedback is you. Help others know how to get the best out of you, and how to help you learn and grow by sharing your preferences around how you best receive feedback.

Session 6: Challenge of WE – Being in Fellowship

Read Chapters 5 & 6 of TFTF and think about a relationship in your own life where you each think the other needs to change. Do the exercise included in "STARTERS" beforehand so that you can answer any questions about it.

It is reasonable to ask: "What's the difference between this session the session on Blind Spots?" In both we look at the ways in which we need each other – in relationship and in fellowship – in order to learn. Session 4 looks at why we need others in order to see ourselves. Others have access to information about us that we can't see on our own, such as facial expressions or the impact our words or actions have on them. Session 6 turns to two topics: (1) the ways we react to the messenger rather than the message, and (2) situations where it's the relationship itself that is often *creating* the feedback. We each think the other person is the problem and it's the other person who needs to change. Some of what we can learn in that process might include behavior that's in our own blind spot – true. But this session takes a deeper look at the interactive nature of relationship systems.

Main Messages

1. We often have a bigger reaction to who is giving us the feedback, than we do to the feedback itself. Often, particularly in relationships with friction, we each think the other person is the problem, and the other person needs to change. Stepping back to see how we are each contributing to the problem can help us

understand the feedback, and learn from the challenges embedded in these relationships.

2. Jesus's message was often rejected because of who he was (or who the listeners believed him to be) so that his message fell on deaf ears.

3. Jesus urges us to see our relationships with each other as mirroring our relationship with God, and our Fellowship together as essential to spiritual growth. Seeing the speck in others' eye is easier than seeing the log in our own.

Session 7: Boundaries

Read Chapter 10 of TFTF and think about your own experience both with drawing boundaries and experiencing the boundaries that others have drawn that impact you. In what ways have your relationships changed in the process of seeking healthier boundaries?

Talking about boundaries can involve talking about challenging relationships and dynamics. This is a good time to refresh the Group Guidelines for Rich Discussion, especially around holding each other in compassion, respecting confidentiality, and not jumping to advising others – help create and maintain healthy boundaries around feedback offered and received within the group.

Main Messages

1. Boundaries are essential to every healthy relationship. God rested on the seventh day, and Jesus routinely withdrew from the crowds and refused to be influenced by the taunts of others.

2. Just because someone offers or wants to offer you feedback does not mean you have to take it. It may not be wise to take it. Saying "no" to some feedback is a way of letting your yes be yes and your no be no (James 5:12).

Session 8: Embracing the Growth Identity

Before you lead this session be sure to read Chapter 9 in TFTF and think about your own tendency. Do you tend to be more fixed or do you hold more of a growth identity? Has this changed over time, or does it change from context to context? How does this impact what you assume about your own spiritual growth?

Main Messages

1. As humans, we keep changing. Part of the good news of being a Christian is that the driving force for our growth and change comes not from ourselves, but from how God is working in our lives.

2. Our mindset impacts our response to challenge or failure, and our ability to learn and grow. TFTF points out that how we hold our identity – the story we tell about who we are and whether we can change – profoundly impacts our reaction to feedback (do we hear it as coaching or evaluation?) and our ability to learn from it.

3. This session invites the group to wrestle with our assumptions about transformation, and how they might nudge themselves toward seeing what's possible in terms of their own growth.

Closure

If you are going to keep the group intact for a next study, this is a good time to talk about how you want to use what you have learned about yourselves and each other in order to get the most from the next study.

If the group will be dispersing, invite a conversation about how to hold each other accountable, and follow up on how things are going. You might also invite them to share how they will use their new skills to get the most out of their next study, with *new* Small Group members. What will they share with the group, and invite from others, to maintain the momentum of their learning?

About the Authors

Sheila Heen is a Founder of Triad Consulting and a faculty member at Harvard Law School. She is a co-author of two *New York Times* bestsellers, *Thanks for the Feedback* (with Douglas Stone) and *Difficult Conversations: How to Discuss What Matters Most* (1999, with Douglas Stone and Bruce Patton). She grew up in Nebraska in the Evangelical Free church and now lives in a farmhouse in New England with her husband and three children.

Elaine Lin is a Senior Consultant with Triad Consulting, and a graduate of Harvard Law School. She works with clients around the world to develop communication and conflict management skills. She grew up in a non-denominational bilingual church in the San Francisco Bay Area, has been part of church communities on three continents, and has a passion for genuine fellowship.

About You

If you found *Thanks for the Feedback* and this workbook helpful, we recommend reading *Difficult Conversations: How to Discuss What Matters Most*, by Stone, Patton & Heen. It provides a next step in strengthening your skills in having the (tough) conversations that matter in your most important relationships, both personal and professional.

For free resources to support your learning, visit:

www.triadconsultinggroup.com under "help yourself"

www.speckbooks.com under "help yourself"

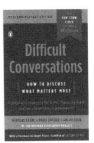

Please share your insights and suggestions with us, so we can incorporate your coaching into later editions of this guide, and allow others to benefit from your experience.

You can send your observations — anything that you found helpful, and suggestions for improvement — to us at feedback@speckbooks.com

Made in the USA
San Bernardino, CA
14 February 2017